the Mominator

WRITTEN BY
Julie Boye

ILLUSTRATED BY
Brooke Knight

ISBN-13: 978-1-7338465-1-6

Published by The Boye Family Jewels

Cover design by Brooke Knight

Typeset by Chelsea Jackson

Edited by Chelsea Jackson, Jackson Writing and Editing, LLC

To the most powerful
Mominators in my life—My mom,
Bonnie, and sisters, Emily, Melissa, Becky,
and Kellie.
To my Mominators-to-be—Adanna, India, and Kenia.
And to the guy who made me a
Mominator—Alex!

Julie

To learn more about Julie, visit mominators.com or @theboyefamilyjewels on Instagram and YouTube.

To my mom, my sister
Chelsea, and my boys, Emmett, Adler, and
Riggs, who all make my mom
life so much fun!

Brooke

To learn more about Brooke, visit @brookeknightillu on Instagram.

Have you ever been *scared* or even been *dared* to do a backflip on a *beam*?

Have you ever felt *small* and not very *tall* but wished you were part of the *team*?

Have you
been
on *stage*
and tried to
be *brave*
but secretly
wanted to
hide?

Did you hope you would *win*, though your chances were *slim*, and got so upset that you *cried*?

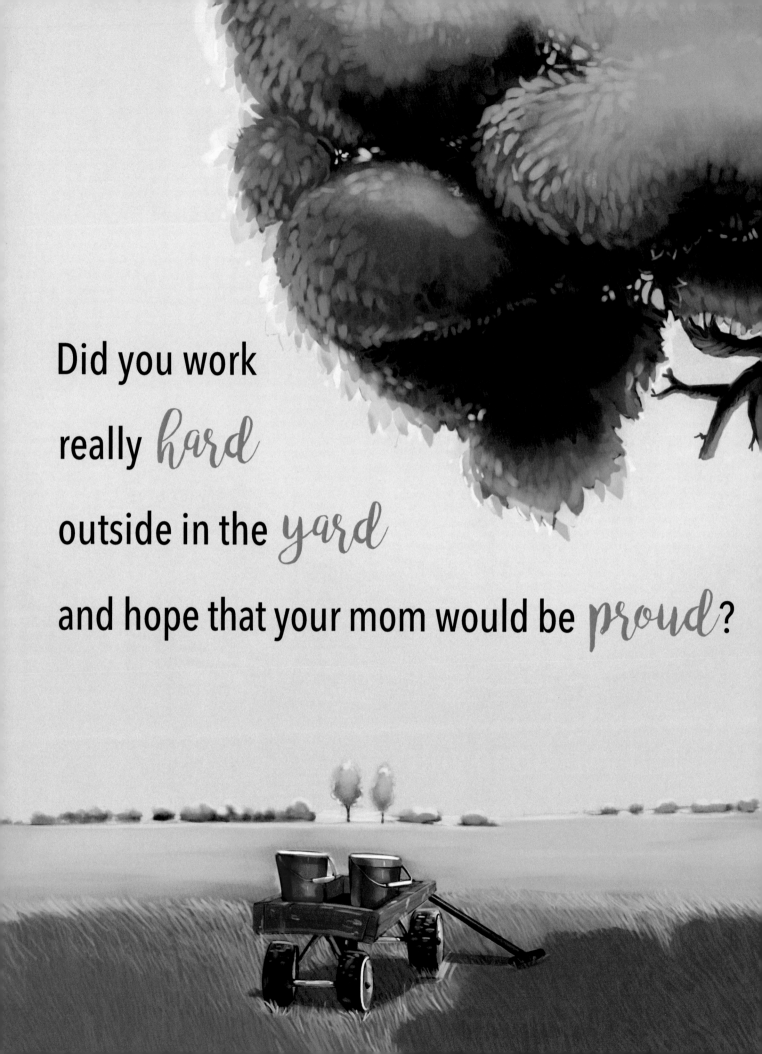

Did you work really *hard* outside in the *yard* and hope that your mom would be *proud*?

Or go out the *door* to play and *explore,* but the snow had already been *plowed?*

Do you feel really *weak* because your *physique* is small and you're not very *strong*?

Did you take a big *test* and feel really *stressed*, hoping none of your answers were *wrong*?

Were you trying to *hurry* but started to *worry* you couldn't quite get to the *potty*?

Have you screamed in the **night** from a terrible **fright** and begged to be cuddled and **held**?

Did you enter a *race* in hopes of first *place*, but you slipped

There's one special *person* who's always *rehearsin'* the best way to help you *succeed*.

She works night and *day* and smiles when you *play*,

and she'll be there for every *nosebleed*!

She'll swaddle and *coo* and clean mountains of *poo* till she thinks that she's going *insane*.

She always seems *tired* but somehow *inspired* to help when you're in a *pickle*.

Her fuse can be *short*—she might yell and *snort*—but she'll take a deep breath and then *tickle*.

She worries and *frets* and usually *sweats* when challenges seem really *tricky*. She can cook. She can *clean*. A multitasking *machine*! She'll be strong when you're both feeling *icky*.

And though there are *times* when moms need to *whine* cuz they feel they can't get it *right*, they're trying their *best*, all moms can *attest* while sleep-training their babies at *night*.

Mom has the *skills* to help you with *drills*. She plays hard, and she dribbles with *vigor*.

She's got your *back*. When you're hurt, she'll *attack* cuz she's strong and her muscles are *bigger*.

The laundry, the dishes, the long Christmas wish list can quickly make her feel *defeated*.

A baby's cute *laughter*
and chocolate right *after*
is usually just
what she *needed*.

No one works *harder*
to help you get *smarter*.
She tries even when she's *impatient*.

When you're growing too *fast* and the time has gone *past*,

she looks in the mirror and feels *ancient*.

Her heart might just *burst* if you win last or *first*. She's proud of you most just for *tryin'*.

She carpools to *school*,

wearing spit-up and *drool*,

and on your first day,

she'll start *cryin'*!

She's the quickest toy *sorter*

and your greatest *supporter*.

She cheers when you need it the *most*.

by eight, she needs peace from the Holy Ghost.

She'll teach you good *manners*.
She's got lots of *planners* for
schedules cuz mom brain is real!

She's forgiving and
kind even when you don't *mind*.

When she's tired of standing, she'll *kneel.*

When she's all out of *love* and needs help from *above*, she's driven by something much *greater*.

Her village of *friends*

and the angels He *sends*

make her a fearless

Mominator!

Julie Boye is the O.G. Mominator. With seven children, ages nine and younger, and a traveling husband, she relates to all different mothers trying to keep their heads above water. Julie is a stay-at-home mom and an out-of-home real-life person (though her kids might not think that) with goals and ambitions. She loves animals, ice cream, and tornadoes, and in her spare time...oh wait, she has no spare time! *Mominator* is her first book.

Brooke Knight is a mom of three young energetic boys. She began art classes at age nine after begging her mom for a year. She studied traditional art under several local artists in Utah. She made the switch to digital and found her niche for illustration, which was a better fit while juggling mommy life. Aside from drawing and mom stuff, she likes to play pickleball and soccer, enjoys Indie folk music, going on walks, and reading to her boys. Oh and devouring almond butter!

43839030R00033

Made in the USA
Middletown, DE
29 April 2019